RAISED FROM SCRATCH

An Inspirational Autobiography
By, Demontae Thompson

ISBN-13: 978-1468093933
ISBN-10: 1468093932

Artwork: Rachael Dinsmore

Demontae Thompson c/o Message Media Ed Publications
4923 W. Adams Blvd.
Los Angeles, Ca 90016
www.MessageMediaEd.org
info@messagemediaed.org

www.RaisedFromScratch.tumblr.com

First Edition

I will do

all things

through God

who strengthens me.

Chapter 1: Do What's Right?

I've come to realize that I don't give myself the credit I deserve. A few years ago a young scholar by the name of Pamela Akametula told me, "Know your worth." I didn't understand what she meant until recently. I didn't understand the meaning of helping others or why I possessed an extra handful of hospitality.

I've done good deeds like helping older women carry their groceries; feeding the homeless who sit shivering, unwelcome in markets or restaurants; helping a boy back onto his bike after a hard fall. I do these things not because I want to be praised or because I want some sort of *Good Samaritan* award. I do them because I believe the inner good within us is sometimes camouflaged by awkward circumstances and because we wonder, "what if?" If at any time I had asked "what if" before I helped someone in distress, I wouldn't have had the courage to do whatever I did. What if the wise lady thinks I'm trying to steal from her? What if the homeless guy tries to infect me with needles? What if the child thinks I'm trying to kidnap him or her? These would have been the thoughts running through my head as I walked away. I could easily pass up a chance to save, to impact, to encourage, to change the past, present, and future generations.

My actions are guided by my conscience. Not too long ago I found a wallet in the grass by the basketball courts here at Cal State University, Northridge, where I'm now a sophomore. I'm not sure what anyone else's first instinct would be, but mine was to take a quick look inside for any cash. One-hundred and fifty-four dollars was folded with a keen crease, similar to my old uniform khakis. I felt richer for a moment; truthfully it looked like a new horizon for me. I tried to think of excuses I would say when I gave the wallet back to its owner like, "There was no money in the wallet when I found it... I didn't even look inside the wallet," etc. All of this could have been avoided if I would have just left the wallet where I'd found it.

I knew whatever I decided to do that an inconspicuous friend named "Karma" would chase after me like my uncle did when I got caught playing with water balloons in the house. I said to myself out loud, "If I'd lost my wallet it would be a blessing to get it back and a miracle within that blessing for it to have all contents present." Skeptically contemplating, I decided to give the wallet back. I contacted the owner who happened to be a coordinator for a program I was interested in. He stood at average height, a middle-aged Latino man. I can still visualize the uncertain joy in his face as he walked toward me when I gave it back to him. He embraced me with gratitude and awe. He said to me, "You are truly a blessing from above, thank you so much."

It was unclear the effect I had on him. I had a sense of, "doing what anybody else would do" in my blood. I didn't think of it as such a big deal until I thought about the hassle he would have to replace his cards and I.D's. I also thought about the money he could use to feed his family and pay bills. Tangible or not, I gave someone I didn't know a learned lesson and a blessing. I believe , if you treat others the way you would like to be treated, you will have a prosperous life; maybe not with wealth but with love, peace, happiness and freedom. We can give the world nourishment if we allow ourselves to nourish others with small actions. Our experiences also assist us in building our identities. Doing what is right is a significant part of mine.

Who Am I?

Permit me to introduce myself!
I am that undeniable statistic of the foster youth.
I am that young man who seems to surpass all negative situations and
impediments.
I am that first time voter who is eager to make a difference in the world with my
opinionated passions.

The agonizing pit of oppression my race has endured, has given me the
strength and courage to be more resilient than the rest
I am a Black boy, who neglects to validate stereotypes others may think I
possess.
With much to say, I am the difference in every open-minded individual, from
those past and forgotten to those near the sound of my voice

I hope to be an adept mentor of life, who provides communities with network
and guidance
But we must know, for those who repel the cry of the untrained youth ironically
repel themselves
To foreshadow the events of glory, God shall give the leaders their dreams and
then some.
I do not confess to my own self that my soul will be departing from the page
unpainted without my permission, but I do however listen to the strokes of life
that may provide answers to my unquestionable doubts.

I am the driven student who will uplift my generation, to rejuvenate their minds
to become the new entrepreneurial activists for life and equality
Men and women are the dependent clauses of civility and without their
commitment to one another, we would cease to exist

So, with a princess on my side to show me the world in a woman's perspective,
she will raise me further up the latter to find the cure for cancer, the home to
the homeless, the life to an embryo and the short constructive responses each
heart desires with the help of God for fulfillment

I am the blood within the vessels that encourage the hearts of others,
I am the eternal love everyone needs to appreciate the gifts of life,
the historical figure that has influenced human race to rebuke lethal situations
the nutrients in the water that runs from the pipes of Beverly Hills to the less
fortunate in Haiti

I am the king of all solutions and a warrior of God's word.
I am your friend and
I am ever faithful,
Inspiration

Chapter 2: Nourishment

Being in my mother's embryonic sac, I swam comfortably for months without any worries. Surprisingly, I had my twin brother swimming along with me. I'm sure I thought life had begun when we were still in my mom's stomach wrestling, but I was wrong. Life began on April 26th to be exact in the year of 1992. There was an alarm that went off to get us out of there, and then I started to get pushed to the light. Unexpectedly my brother grabbed me by my ankle and pulled me back down so he could come out first. I guess that was his way of paying me back for depriving him of food. That's why he's the smaller and older twin. The doctor didn't have to smack us on the behind because he didn't have a free hand.☺ My brother and I are considered mirror-image identical twins; put us directly in front of each other and we are mere reflections. Opposite features like which hand we write with, our hair texture and our teeth are characteristics that make us mirror-image. Unfortunately, they discovered drugs in my mother's system and took us away. She probably didn't get a chance to hold us. She must have been devastated. ☹

I was raised in Compton, California, a small ghetto city next to Watts and Long Beach. I lived in an old neighborhood in the back of Martin Luther King Hospital, also known as "Killer King". It acquired this nickname because this was the closest hospital to our community that could not accommodate the high volume of patients due to gang violence and casualties.

In my neighborhood, each house had its own style and flavor like starburst candy. It is a residential area with palm trees sprinkled scenically behind each home. The houses owned history. Most of the home owners were black couples whom retired to enjoy the American dream, while the rest of them were on their way. Some houses had paint chipping from window panes while others had the best stucco money could buy. The ice cream trunk would come by at the same time each day. The smell in the air on my street was always incredibly fulfilling because each house's food aromas would escape from their front doors into the streets.

I don't think any home had any gates or fences around the front yards, but I do know that many of them had dogs in their back yards for unwanted visitors. All homes on my block had to have bars around their window due to burglaries. The sidewalks were for kids. We couldn't go in the street and the grass, so we made the driveways and sidewalks our best friends. When it was hot we would lay on them to dry off and when it was cold we would have puddle-splashing contests. I know now why the streets weren't ours, because gang members and bad kids would be in them; riding their bikes, driving mopeds and causing trouble. Their cars sped through our streets as fast as the basketballs being thrown at the broke down courts. I knew the saying, "*If you look for trouble, you'll find it*" and I didn't want no trouble. It was quiet when the sun was out, but when darkness came, darkness came. I've heard strange noises like cats fighting and dogs barking, and gunshots and fireworks were indistinguishably normal to me. I slept with fear in my eyes. One night I heard tires screech and gunshots blast like bass in the hip hop music my family listened to. As I awoke with sweaty palms and shivering legs I walked trembling to the bathroom. I couldn't go back to sleep due to the fear of someone coming into our house killing my family. That was my first all-nighter. That night, our "hood" was attacked by gang rivals. The following day, I overheard my neighbors talking about someone getting shot 3 times and announced critical in the hospital.

Early in my childhood, I didn't know the meaning of having a twin. I wondered why this boy looked and acted like me and went everywhere I went. All I knew was regardless if I fail or succeeded; he was there to lift me up for some reason. We grew closer to each other as we matured. I had him to confide in. He was always there for yelling, laughing, fighting and playing. He was and still is my best friend, brother and competitor. He keeps me on my toes whenever I feel like slacking. When life gets confusing, I hear him say, "What are you doing stupid?" I know what ever I do in life I have to do with passion, cause if I don't I know he'll call me out on it. Even though we are twins we have different personalities.

We have different ways of seeing things. He sees thing for what they are and I see things for what they could be. With our differences we argue and fight like nobody's business. I mean fist fighting, name-calling and pushing each other to our limits. We knew not to fight in public because that would make us look bad. When we did fight, I'd say I won and he'd say he won. If he made me laugh when we were upset with each other, we squashed the whole thing and forget about it. We'd share money or food as well. We knew that our love for one another could never cease. I can surely say that without him in my life I could not function. I always had a vision about him or me separating from one another, but never gave it much thought. There would be times when we'd go to different states alone and I would miss his nagging and curiosity. I now know,

> *If someone inquires about your life, that means they care and want to see how they fit in the picture or how they can help.*

It's not to be nosey or to just start conversation. If you have the opportunity, take that conversation to the next level and expand your understanding on where you'd like to go in life. Since my twin and I spoke and listened to one another with respect and sincerity, we had no problem speaking to others. Your communication starts to flourish when you begin with the ones you respect the most.

However, in some circumstances I regret being a twin. One day at our middle school, Willowbrook, my brother had a girlfriend and was in love. I was walking to lunch with hunger in one hand and anticipation in the other. One of my brother's friends approached me with negativity and confusion. She said, "Why did you make your girlfriend cry?" I replied, "What girlfriend, what are

14

you talkin'...?" Before I could speak another word she slapped me on my face. My whole head turned away from her due to the force she had, and it whipped back around with a demonic expression. I got angry to the point where I contemplated hitting her back, but I didn't. I looked directly in her eyes and exclaimed, "I'm not my brother, what did you hit me for?" She immediately apologized. "I'm sorry Tae, oh, I'm so sorry", as she giggled. I stood there looking ridiculous and gave a smirk. Before I left, she hugged me and smiled. I don't know if it was the apology or the hug that made me feel better. When I saw my brother, a part of me wanted to slap him, but I just laughed about it. He laughed hysterically because he knew what happened before I could explain it. I told him, "Bro, you need make sure you don't do anything crazy or spiteful because people are gonna think you are me and I don't want to hurt nobody." LOL He laughed and agreed, "Yea I know, I don't want your friends coming up to me slapping me, shoot." From that day on we had a few guidelines for one another: There will be times where people will get us confused and that we must do the right things so we won't get punished for each other's actions. I still get questions like, "Were you the guy that was dancing in the pool?" I'd have to get my thoughts together for two minds and respond, "I don't think I was at any pool, you might be thinking of my twin brother." The person would then be in disbelief and say, "Yea right!" Then I'd show them a picture and laugh at the whole conversation. Some people can tell the difference.

Now he's skinnier and shorter than I am. Even though it might be half of an inch and a few pounds, these differences make us distinguishable. However, most times my family would just call us twin and whichever one of us would come they'd be satisfied or they'd just say, "Where the other one at, tell him to come here?"

I grew to know that my parents weren't ever around for us. I wonder sometimes if my parents ever had any remorse for abandoning their kids, or did they just live day to day encouraged by their satisfaction of being high. What

runs through their heads when they think of one of us?
What do they tell themselves? It's gonna get better, I'm
gonna turn my life around or I'd be better off without them.
I wish I could tell them *"history is created everyday lived,
but you shouldn't live every moment regretting history."*

Invisible

What is the difference between like and love?

I've tried to figure this out on many occasions.

My invisible mom told me that if I find love to never let it go because people are out here dying in search for that word.

Thoughts rolled off my mind like, how am I supposed to hold on to something if I don't even know what it is? And why can't love just come and go like police in the ghetto arresting kids for stealing bubble gum from the candy house, meanwhile the loud neighbors next door are steady whooping the life out of their foster kids with extension cords and tree limbs.

"Sorry little Tim, I hear your screams but I play as If they're just laughter created from the T.V. Screens, and when I see you on the street I just can't help but to think, what the heck happened to YO head?"

Instead I think of ways you've might have fallen, like from a bunk bed.

Another question is, if you get beat does that mean your parents care?

I heard from other people that love hurts, but if love hurts should you die to love or die for love?

My invisible dad told me that love doesn't exist in a man's world, so I said who rule the world, Girls?

He gave me this sarcastic look for some reason, so I smiled and walked away.

And thought, "If this world were mine..."

Sometimes it feels like no one has ever showed me what love should look like.

Sometimes stare in my computer screen on Facebook, and ask friends to like my status. Love is a myth, we try to satisfy someone that might not even like us because we get butterflies in our tummies and those feelings that we get ain't merely a glimpse of reality.

Have you ever said I love you to someone with tears on your cheeks, with your eyebrows dipped low, or with bruises on your heart from tribulations? Cuz I have. Many other foster kids had it worse.

Violently worse.

This fairy tale of a world will forever be locked up in chains, taking cruises around my life like its shuttled into space. The moon doesn't exist, the sun isn't so hot, and red means go and green means stop.

One more petal on the sunflower, I love my parents or maybe I love them not.

How can you love someone who wasn't even there?

I understand that I can't rewind the time to make my history with my parents more appealing and less hurtful, but I'd give the world to have a complete family one day. I don't think that day will come until I create one on my own, but I do know if I take action now, my future with my parents will be more fulfilling. My thoughts of aggression and gloom were created from the absence of my parents. I grew up with other kids asking me, "why I never seen yo parents", and I would reply back by saying, "I don't get in trouble so they don't have a reason for coming to the school". I kept the fact that I didn't live with my parents from other children because I knew what they would say. They would have picked on me until my self-esteem was as small as a watermelon seed. I did realize that many people took their parents for granted. I always heard some friends say, "I hate my mom. She's always bossing me around and in my business." I knew that when parents are in your business that means they care, but I didn't tell them that I just shook my head and smiled. I never made references to anyone about how nosey my parents were, because I didn't want anybody in my business, and I would actually prefer nosey parents over living without them. Knowing that mostly all the guys I knew had their parents to answer certain questions like, "Why is the sky blue? What do I say to girls?" etc., made me feel like I was hiding in a box of solitude. I would sometimes live life day-by-day thinking, "What if my parents return? I had a frown on my face all the time while growing up. People who met us immediately called me the evil or bad twin. Why should I smile when I had so much to process inside? I always wanted to fight. I guess fighting my twin before we were born must have been foreshadowing. I don't know how but I thought looking mad made me cute. I always fought for being number one at everything. When I lost I wanted a rematch. There was something about me that made me different than the rest of the kids.

When I was in 4th grade, I had a devilish encounter. Being the class clown I was the center of attention. On this particular day, I wore new shoes. The chalkboard was clean and fresh and the whole class was working in groups. My best friend at the time, Travion, and a few more students, were sitting next to me. Travion was my partner in crime so he and I were isolated from the group doing our own thang. I took the jelly beads from my shoes and put them on the table. As I opened them I noticed how edible they looked. I said to Travion, "Look at these beads." He told me, "Oh these are tight." I then murmured, "Give them to Jasmine and tell her that they're Nerds (candy)." Being that he was as bad as I was, he did it. I heard her make an argument as I turned my head to play it off. She called the teacher over to the table and my little joke became serious. Mrs. Weatherspoon took the beads and threw them in the trash as she demanded me to come to her desk. I knew I was in trouble because of the tone of her voice. I remember her telling the class, "Y'all gone make me lose my mind, up in here, up in here," whenever we got loud. She said, "What if Jazmine would have eaten those beads? Then what would you have done?" A tear fell from my left cheek as I began to understand that I could have killed her. I had to go apologize to her and pick up the rest of the tiny beads from the floor. I got suspended that day for 2 days. The principal told me that this might be on my record when I grow up. She said, "How do you expect to get a job when they see that you tried to poison somebody?" I'm not sure if she was trying to scare me or if she was telling the truth. Since I haven't heard about this incident for about 10 years, I believe she just wanted me to learn a meaningful lesson. I learned that I was really messed up in the head. What made me want to end someone else's life? Did I want others to feel the pain of not having parents as well? ☹

I always dreamt of a sunny day at the park playing catch with a tennis ball with my dad, as my mom chased my brother around the swing set. I owned millions of dreams like these. I also dreamed of asking my mom if I could have a girlfriend and if I was a cute little boy. I would never know because those dreams are lost underneath the absence and silence of the word, "family". A little part of me doesn't believe in family because my definition of family is merely a combination of people who hug you, feed you and leave you. I wanted to believe that this definition could change but it was hard for me. I tried to think of questions to ask my family like, "Where is my mom and dad? How many brothers and sisters do I really have?" However, I couldn't ask them because they would just look at me stupid and say something like, "Boy, go take a nap." I did however have my uncle and aunt to depend on. I was once a lost, wounded cub. I had to earn my stripes and grow up in the wild before realizing I could make an impression on people's lives. I was raised from my community. My community were the people who surrounded me; the people who knew me on a deeper level.

My guardian and all time inspirational figure in my life is my uncle Lorenzo Edwards. My family and others call him, Uncle Lowe. He was born a day after Christmas. There must have been fate for him to be born on that date and to own angel-like qualities. He is an honorable man because he helps everyone in the neighborhood with construction, respects the community and takes care of his family. Uncle Lowe is now 87 years old. He has dark, gleaming skin, with grey hair on his head usually covered by baseball caps. He also has strong, stretched cheeks sometimes filled with chewing tobacco. Unlike in any other foster home I could have been sent to as an infant, I was very fortunate and blessed to have been welcomed into his house with loving arms, along with three other siblings. Being in foster care with my great uncle, gave him a chance to teach me as he would teach his son. I'd call him Daddy sometimes to show him that I appreciate the care and nourishment he provided. He was a man who did things his way because he knew it would get done and done right.

I can recall the times he would tell me, "Get the crescent wrench out of the bucket." I always got it mixed up with the pliers for some reason. I would bring him the pliers and he would scream at me, "Didn't I tell you to get the crescent wrench, not the damn pliers, listen to me when I tell you something." I was much smaller I didn't know better. He always went hard on me. Whenever I started to act lazy he would say, "You will never be able to keep a job." These words will be forever remain in my head because of the amount of times I've heard it. I couldn't wait to grow up and prove him wrong. He would see one day that that I'd be the best employee an employer ever hired. This was a unique form of motivation: reverse psychology.

Although I was raised in Compton, I wasn't raised by Compton. I wasn't influenced by any activity in my neighborhood. One of the lessons my uncle taught me was how to respect adults. Many times there would be visitors for Uncle Lowe who I did not recognize at the door. I would just let them in. I still remember him standing there with his dark, shiny skin glowing from the morning sun and his superior, deep voice exclaim, "When company comes in, you have this house clean and you offer them something to eat or drink and from now on that's what you do!" I did not understand why we were giving our food away to these people, but as I grew, I figured it out. It was courtesy and hospitality. Uncle Lowe would yell, "Twin, didn't I tell you to cut that grass." I would then respond, "No you told the other twin," with a smirk on my face because I honestly

22

knew it was me. He would go on and on about how he told one of us to cut the grass. Then would sit me down on the plastic covered couch and say, "When I or another adult tells you to do something, you don't do what you want to do, you do what is asked of you. If you respect people, people gonna respect you." I felt remorse clogging up my throat. I knew he was serious because he would spit his tobacco in a paper cup after every sentence and look me directly into my eyes. I looked back at him with eyes filled with tears and said, "I understand."☹ I walked away slowly and began to mow the lawn. From that day forward I respected not only adults, but my family, my friends, and myself. In my life, learning the hard way and being supervised throughout assisted me in making my future satisfying.

In my household, education was extremely important. Uncle Lowe's wife, Verna Mae Edwards was a dark skinned, southern heritage woman who always wore clothes and accessories I've never seen before and cooked better food than anyone I knew. Due to cancer I never got to connect deeper with her because angels took her away to a better place in 2002. Before she passed she told my uncle to be sure that my brother and I got through school. For the most part, growing up and going to school was easy and fun. However, when I started high school it got rough. I obtained a job at McDonalds in 2008 after my 16th birthday and thought I could work and still keep good grades. I thought wrong. I made money, became popular in school, and I had a 1975 Buick Century with cream beige paint, brown leather interior and, white wall tiers. My life was great in my mind until my progress report was sent to my house.

I got in from school that day and got the lecture of my life. As I approached the table my uncle sat there silent with my report card in his hand. I knew there was something wrong. He asked me, "Who this here report card?" I responded softly, "Mines." Before I could give an explanation for my grades he began to curse and yell. Screaming, "What the HELL you thinking? Every since you got that car and job you went wild." I had nothing to say. He continued, "Back in my day, I got an ass whooping for every D and F I got in school. I should park that car in the back. You need to stop messin' around and focus on school; that car girls and money gone come later." I knew what he was saying but I was also confused because he was the one who demanded me to get a job and car. Eventually I took what he said into consideration.

I always tried to make my uncle proud of me. When my brother and I were younger we assisted him on many jobs. These jobs were not easy. We helped him put in windows, lay concrete slabs and remodel the structure of houses. Moving huge rocks made it seem like indentured servitude. He'd always say, "Don't strain yourself", but he would always make us do the work of men. I didn't get it. I remember the times when we were working in my cousin's complex and he would talk to us about how he built a pool for a park in Compton and how he worked in Alaska for 3 days in a row because he didn't know that the sun stayed out for months at a time in the summer time. He is a wealthy man with two trucks, 4 bedroom house and an acre of property in Warren, Arkansas. He is what I call successful, happy, and retired.

One day before going to work, Uncle Lowe took my brother and I to the store. When we left the store my brother was rushing to the car. Uncle Lowe said to him," "Why you in such a rush and what's that in yo' pocket?" I stood there quiet even though I knew what it was. I could see the fear sweating from his face. My brother murmured, "Some candy." Uncle Lowe said, "What you stealing for? I buy y'all everything y'all want and y'all shouldn't have a reason to take nothing from any stores. What you gone do, is go back into that store, put that candy back where you got it from and apologize." My brother was crying and I actually felt as bad as he did. After that incident my uncle talked to us the whole ride home. He said, "If you want something you have to ask for it, don't be scared; a closed mouth doesn't get heard and a close mouth doesn't get fed. I don't wanna ever see or hear about yall stealing again. You gotta work for everything you want like I did. I came to California with no more than fifty cents in my pockets and look at what I got. I worked for it and I didn't steal from anybody." It got me to think at that time, why is life so hard? As I grew up my uncle taught me that if life isn't hard, then you're not doing something right. I thought about this every day. I know that if I'm going to school and working, "doing everything right", I would still have challenges in my life I use what he has been instilled in my mind and soul to work hard to overcome those challenges, never steal, and focus on what I need to do. Live life to the fullest.

I will never let anything get in the way of my success because I know he taught me better than that. If I was never put in foster care I would have never obtained so much love, knowledge and wisdom from a man who is someone more than a guardian/great uncle, but a father figure. Every young boy needs an Uncle Lowe in their lives to have a successful transition into manhood. My Uncle wasn't the only one who raised me. My teachers and neighbors also invested in me. They had so much faith in a young man at such a young age, it made me feel special because at home I didn't get as much attention as I'd liked.

Across the stress from where I lived, was a family who owned foster children too. Conception and Earnest were a well established Black couple. They had super hearts for children. I remember them buying all the children on the street ice cream. I was around 7 or so, but I would still run over to them and thank them, since ice cream didn't exist in my house-hold. My uncle told my sister, twin and I, "I don't ever wanna see ya'll running to an ice cream truck, don't make them rich off of the lil' change ya'll need to be saving." ☹ Oooh! I hated him for that. Then I got over it and took advantage of all the cookies and cakes that was in the house. I would take the cookies out the cookie jar and smile with crumbs on my face when everyone wondered where they had gone. LOL. The cool couple across the street would sometimes call my brother and I over for savoring root beer floats and other snacks. They would treat us like we were their children. Sometimes they would say, "These are my twins", and we would just go with the flow. Earnest would teach us about making money and Conception would teach us about life.

Every summer starting in 2005, KeKe (my sister), Tray and I went with Uncle Lowe to Arkansas to visit his side of the family. His brother, J.D. Edwards lived in the town of Warren with his wife Betty Edwards. J.D. would see my brother and I and ask us, "What are yall grades for yall lessons", with a country accent. We would bring our report cards and "A" papers to show him. He rewarded us with candy and money. I'm not sure if it was a lot, but at that time, a little was a lot to us. J.D. and his wife were so beautiful. He wore a jerry curl on his head. He had a shiny, and sun-bright gold tooth in his mouth too. Now, Betty always had the best looking hair, I've ever seen on a woman. I believe it was an "up do" with pinned curls. Even though her hair was a young grey color, it was creative and always intriguing. They had adult sons, and daughters. One that I can remember was named Lucinda. She always had an African style, from her hair to her clothing. She had Betty's eyes, the kind of eyes that would see the mundane as extraordinary. Tray and I attended her wedding to Donald in 2006. He was a smart old ma, and he would always crack jokes. Being in Arkansas for a few weeks gave us an experience of a life-time. Out there, they valued pecans more than they did the shoes they wore. They made their lives exciting, with what they had. I'm not sure I'd live in such a rural environment, but I know for sure that I'll be visiting soon.

What Tray and I took from these trips was the idea that we loved candy and money. We knew that money wasn't going to be handed to us; we had to search for it. Since all the candy in Arkansas was cheap, my brother and I saved up all of our money one year to get all the candy we wanted. We planned how we were going to hide the candy from Uncle Lowe because we knew, in our right minds, that he wouldn't allow us to take it back to California. That summer, we arrived at the store called, Dollar General, and contemplated on our selection and strategy. We decided to buy the candy that was "10 for a dollar" and come back to California to sell them for a quarter a piece. We bought around 80 dollars worth of goodies that day. Conception and Earnest always told us, "Start young and think smart because your future is closer than you think". We returned from Arkansas and took what we learned from everyone we knew and started a candy store. We couldn't go to the ice cream trucks, so we decided to have our own ice cream. Our store was called, The Twins One-Stop-Shop. Being that the ice cream truck had a route and circuit to follow we knew the kids on our street would truly benefit from our stop. We sold chocolates, juices, pop cycles, and a variety of other fruity candy. On our first day on the job, Conception was our first costumer. She asked us questions about the prices and deals so we would be prepared for other costumers. She always said, "Money can be the root to all evil, so be careful okay twins" and I believed her. While she assisted us, people down the street started to walk down and check us out. We eventually had people stopping their cars to support us. We considered ourselves to be businessmen. That day was a success; we cleaned up, counted our money and made flyers for the next day. We made 60 dollars and 45 cents that day. Tray always kept the money because he knew how to be frugal and wise with it. Meanwhile, I'd try to eat some of the surplus merchandise. We weren't headed for the stars, we were headed for the sun; the biggest star in out sight. Uncle Lowe was even proud of us! He would tell his friends, "My boys made 60 dollars out there selling candy." Even though he'd never said, I'm proud of ya'll", we just knew he was. At the end of it all, our shop grew and our relationship with Uncle Lowe grew. He would love to hear from us at the end of each day. He'd say, "How ya'll do today", and we'd respond in our squeaky voices simultaneously, "It went good, we made more than we made yesterday."

We were 15 and impervious to insults like, "The twins gonna grow up to sell Kool-Aid for a living," or even, "The twins think they tight because they got a little candy house." In reality, everyone in our community supported us, buying some candy or giving donations. We grew mentally and when we asked Uncle Lowe for something, *sometimes* he'd get it for us, which was huge. However, in his eyes, we still had a lot of growing up to do.

The shoes we wore were always leaning to one side or had holes at the bottom of them. One time we asked Uncle Lowe for shoes for school and he said, "Yall better use the ones you have" and we'd say, "But they got holes in 'em". He then exclaimed, "Then go barefoot then. I use to go to school in paper bags." We didn't know what to say after that. We thought he was just playing but he was serious. That taught us to be empathetic to others who couldn't afford even the little that we had. A few months later after having wet socks from water puddles and hiding our holes from our friends, he took us to payless. None of our friends shopped at payless, because their shoes weren't name brand. We got the closest name brand shoe in the store, some Shaq's. We loved Shaq's because they were cheap and they look a bit like Jordan's. Uncle Lowe taught us, when we have to pay for our own necessities, then we would begin to understand that name-brand doesn't matter. The days when were making and keeping our own money was the day when we started to save. We started a bank account when we were 16. The banker who started it for us, Oscar Rodriguez, is our humble mentor to this day.

Seemingly, the people that I've met, connected with, or even spoken to have influenced me drastically. Even though, my circumstances put barriers in my way, I was *Raised From Scratch*, transforming from fragile pieces of insecurities to a humble, wise young man.

In order to live a great life you must place all discouragements in the TRASH BIN, click the START button to begin an exploration for nourishment and RESTART your journey from that point on. Let the family connections and friendships you build help you get across the bridge of life. No one is capable of living without help. Nurture your mind with knowledge to prepare for the future.

Chapter 3: It Happens for a Reason

If God gave me one wish, I would wish for more time. If I had more time to do things I'm passionate about, I could give more effort and make sure my long and short-term goals were met. Many people are afraid of dying and of what might happen in the future. I've learned that,

> *Being afraid and being excited are the same feelings; sweaty palms, heart racing with anticipation. Therefore, we should not be afraid of dying but excited to live.*

Not knowing the future gives us an opportunity to begin our quests to find our purpose, identity and self-worth. Inquiring about life and being passionately curious is the key to the door of opportunities, opportunities to live our lives to the fullest.

> *There will be trails, but with every great road trip we should expect to have some bumps in the road.*

I had bumps, when I was much smaller. I didn't know what to do, how to feel and who to ask for help. Sometimes I would create some of my own bumps, which would make me feel like turning around and giving up, but we have to get over our bumps, because if we drive around them, we might end up off-road somewhere where we don't belong.

Before I reached my teen years I was unhappy with my size and wanted to be bigger. Unfortunately there was nothing I could do to make my enemy, "puberty" come any faster. This was a bump like no other. Although my head had not caught up with my body yet, it felt good to be skinny. At least I could run fast from anything that tried to harm me. I had chicken legs and a big smile I didn't look the way I wanted to, but I was blessed to have my health. I used to be the boy who would volunteer at P.E. class to set examples for the other students. I was the type who liked to be among the winning circle. I loved to race and push through physical obstacles. Having a healthy body can provide necessary oxygen and knowledge to your mind, if you let it. I had an interview with a physical struggle around this time in my life. My twin and I had just received bunk beds for the first time in our lives. We were excited like a woman that just said yes to a marriage proposal. We both knew this would make our room spacious so we could have more fun.

One night we were getting ready for bed. My brother called the top bunk, so I had to take the bottom. I thought the bottom bunk was dark and scary. If a monster came out of the closet I would be the first one he'd eat. I feared and hated the bottom bunk and Tray knew that so he allowed me to sleep with him up top. I knew there was something missing from the top bunk, but wasn't sure what it was. Unfortunately, I figured out it was the railing at the top to prevent anyone from falling. Since Tray was sleeping by the wall, I felt vulnerable to the monsters. I'm not sure if it was the monsters or my tossing and turning, but something made me fall 6 feet onto the floor. The fall woke me up. I moaned, groaned and made my way to the bottom bunk as if I was a gofer crawling out from its whole for the first time.

The funny part is, I tried to get away from the monsters and danger, but danger still managed to get me. Now I know,

Meet your fear face to face instead of avoiding it because at some point in time you will unexpectedly be introduced.

I was in agonizing pain and tried to keep it a secret. At that time if I told my family they would take the beds away and if I told my teacher she would probably think something was going wrong at home. With no sleep, I went to school the following morning. My favorite teacher Mrs. Wheatherspoon questioned me about my arm. I wondered how she knew something was wrong. I guess when a student isn't jumping off the walls and joking around like usual, you can take an educated guess or assume that there's something wrong. She said to me, "Demontae what's wrong with you?" I answered, "Nothing". She replied, "I know something is wrong. Is everything okay at home?" At that second I didn't want to say anything because I didn't want her thinking I was getting abused, but I couldn't just stay quiet, so I told her the truth. Sometimes, the truth hurts, but in this instance, it hurt not to tell the truth. She believed me and called my family. I was sent home early with my work. The next day I went to hospital and discovered I dislocated my shoulder! I was given a brace that I had to wear for 6 months. If it wasn't for her I would probably be sitting here now holding on to a painful secret in my left shoulder.

We as people, let minor colds, scratches and bruises affect our futures. We should use these scratches to motivate us. Take a look at any scars you have and believe those scars have given you experience and knowledge. Scars only look bad when you feel insecure about them and don't express the adventurous stories behind them. Take care of yourself and be aware that any given time, you might trip in fall over what life has to offer.

Life may throw punches when you least expect it. When you learn to swing back, that's when you begin to live.

Another bump in my life was introduced before I turned 10. One of my first cousins, Uncle Louis (Uncle

Lowe's son), always had a limp in his walk and was a skinny man. He had only one good leg; I never did know what happened to the other one, until after he passed away in 2005 due to cancer. He was shot in front of our house because he owed someone money and did not pay them back. Every time he took a step, or where ever he'd go, he probably thought about how losing his leg could have been avoided. He had a raspy, old voice. He was skinny like a door and tall as the trees at a park. He used to limp to the back house and take Tray and I to the church near the Nickerson Gardens (the housing projects) every Sunday. I saw this as an opportunity to get a hot meal every week. Sitting in church eating grits with all the sugar I could ask for, sausage and cinnamon toast felt like heaven to me. I only prayed for material things. I didn't know what it meant to worship. What I did know was communion was fun. I thought it was cute the way we collectively ate a little cracker and drank cranberry juice. If you asked me, it was a big tease. I didn't understand the preacher but I knew he was honorable. He would come up to my brother and me, and complement us on our clothes. Other people in the church that knew my uncle would give us money because they said we were nice boys. They didn't even know us☺. Sometimes my uncle would take our money and use it for himself.

Throughout the times we spent with Uncle Lewis, he made our childhood very exciting. He would bribe us with candy and snacks to role with him on a mission. We knew what "a mission" was at the time. It was when he would go to the grocery store and "five-finger discount" some bottled soap. He would put it in a pouch he had attached to his metal leg. One time Uncle Louis told us to watch for people entering the aisle as he stuffed bottles in his pouch. We were the cute little "Look-outs". Eventually it got to a point where he would take us all the time. We were an unexpected team, but the night that changed our lives was when we got caught. There was a security guard dressed in regular clothes that followed us aisle to aisle without being seen; maybe we weren't looking good enough. He approach

Uncle Louis with a deep voice and pulled out his badge and demanded, "Excuse me, can you take a walk with me." Uncle Louis was in shocked and didn't know what to say or do. He took a deep breath and murmured, "I only got one leg", guessing that the security guard would feel some sort of sympathy for him. As the liquid soap fell out of his pouch, people began to look our way. Embarrassment was an understatement. My brother and I didn't know what to do because we didn't know anything else but how to be by our uncle's side and watch out for him. He never prepared us for circumstances of getting caught. So we followed him and the guard into this little room. The guard had him on tape and caught him red handed. I knew we were in trouble. I started to ask myself, "What is jail like for 8 year olds? How am I going to explain this to Uncle Lowe? And I'm too young to die☹." The man let us walk away with no charges, but said, "If I ever catch any of you in this store again stealing you're going to jail." I had a lump in my throat, but I just smiled innocently as I walked out from the store.

Everything happens for a reason. Never will I again be an accomplice to a crime. How wrong is it to take the blame or to be punished for something you didn't do?

> *We will never be set free until we know the full truth, granted, the full truth is sometimes unexplainable.*

Chapter 4: Don't Forget to Look Back

    I was ignorant about a few things in my life and wanted to find answers. My Brother Joey is two years older than I am. He was taller than the rest of us. He kept to himself most of the time. When we were younger we'd play games with him on the Play station and he'd always win. I didn't like that; he could've at least let us win sometimes. He was the "big brother" in the house and had to keep us "little ones" in check whenever we got out of hand. We'd fight because he'd think he was the boss all the time. However, we use to have a lot of fun making jokes of each other and letting our imagination run wild. I remember Joey, KeKe, Tray and I use to make tents outside. Since we'd never been camping, we thought it'd be fun to camp in the back yard. We used sheets and ply- wood, chairs and extension cords to make our tent. We even brought the T.V. out back. We had to look out for Uncle Lowe because we knew he'd have a fit if he caught us fooling around with his tools and dangerous materials. We used a brick to secure the sheets up top, so they wouldn't fly away. We finally finished it all and started to settle in. Then one grey brick fell directly on KeKe's forehead. KeKe already had a bigger than normal forehead; this made it worse. We all laughed as she cried. We tried to help her, but she didn't want help. She ruined the whole afternoon. We had to tear the whole structure down and come inside. It wasn't hard for us to have fun with each other because Uncle Lowe didn't allow us to go over friend's house to play. Eventually we grew apart. KeKe spent more time on the phone than playing with us and Joey reached an age where he'd go out with his friends most of the time. We all began to feud more about simple issues; I think that was our way of saying I love you.

Joey grew up fast and I could see his changes. He use to look over us and take care of us. But he also got to the point where he'd always think we were always in his business. We didn't know him anymore. I always wondered how he thought and why he thought the way he did. When I started the 6th grade, Joey was starting the 8th grade at Willowbrook. I'd walk around the school and see him sometimes, but we never acknowledge each other or sat down to eat lunch or anything. It was like we weren't even brothers. People there would try to pick on me. I heard someone say, "Don't be messing with the twins, those Joey little brothers". I guess Joey had a reputation of some sort. Everyone knew my brother somehow. It hit me one day; Joey didn't want to be seen with us, because he didn't want everyone to know that we were his relatives because they could use that against him. I could be wrong, but I will never know. I do know that he changed my life.

In the year of 2007, as a selection of friends and my entire family danced to R'Kelly's "Steppin' in the Name of Love", something horrible happened. Our house was broken into. Conception arrived at the event and told Uncle Lowe's daughter Tricia, "Tricia! Lowe's house was broken into, come on. I already called the police". We intended to have a great surprise Father's day party for Uncle Lowe around the corner from where we lived, but ended up with vandalized hearts. I felt like a voodoo doll, with a sharp needle in my chest. I left with Uncle Lowe and Tray. When we arrived home, our safe was in the middle of the street off its hinges. As I walked in, I wondered who would take the value and happiness of others for satisfaction. When I got to my room, my games were gone and closet was cleaned out. The weird thing was, there were some outfits left that still had tags on them. They also rummaged through our family pictures as if the theft knew us.

Joey was a prime suspect. He was our brother, but knew where everything was in the house. He was nowhere to be found. I didn't know if he did it or not, but I hated him unequivocally. Uncle Lowe's truck was found at a local park that week with shredded leather and flat tires. I didn't feel safe living there ever since the burglary. I thought monsters only existed when I was younger. Joey was eventually caught and taken to court. I didn't know what he said or how he felt, but he was sentenced about 2 years in a group home, jail-like facility. After the incident, I missed Joey like crazy. Even though he tried to punk us, and I resented him for it, I knew he loved us. After his time was up, he tried to speak to our family, but was rejected. I was told that he was a bad influence and should not speak to him. I didn't know, "blood was thicker than water".

Three years later, I really resented him. He was a corrupt gangster in my eyes. In the middle of 2011, Joey sent me a request on Face book. I contemplated adding him. My curiosity to know the truth helped me press the confirm button. When I added him, I told him to call me and to explain the history that separated us. He called and said, "Bro, it's been a long time". I murmured, "Yea, too long, how are you?" He then started to emphasize he didn't do it. I asked him in a soft tone, "Why did you have to leave us?" He exclaimed he didn't want to. He said, "I didn't take nothing from Uncle Lowe. Some gangsters who were friends with a member of our family did it. They set it all up. I knew who did it, but they told me, if I said anything, they would hurt my family. They would hurt you and Tray and KeKe. My eyes began to tear up with guilt and care. I knew, the young, funny, caring Joey still existed, but I didn't let him exist. He also said that, he tried to apologize to the rest of the family, but they weren't having it. They tore up his letters and pictures he would send us. As I write this book today, I have not seen him in 4 long devastating years. I didn't know whether to believe him or to condemn him. I know that God gave me a chance to have my brother back and I will take advantage of it. ☹

> *Being absent from someone could show you how much of an impact, positive or negative, they had on you.*

I forgave him that night on the phone, and we both said four words I would have never think of saying, "I LOVE YOU BROTHER". I thought he took our valuables, but he didn't, and instead he gave us our lives.

> *It's amazing how our destiny sometimes lies in the hands of people we'd least expect.*

A closed mouth can't verbally express what it needs, that's why we have a voice. We can express what we need to succeed which helps us gain perspectives in life. If we all own this power, we can learn from the mistakes of others. Imagine how enormous one thought can impact a people. Dr. Martin Luther King, Jr. demonstrated this for us. We must always look back on our experiences, thoughts and dreams, and continue to push forward with lessons learned, new understandings and collective action for future generations to follow.

Chapter 5 Epitaph

As of now, at the age of 19, I don't know a fraction of what I feel I should I know. Through experiences and curiosity, I will obtain the necessary knowledge and share it with others. If we do what's right, seek relationships that are nurturing, acknowledge everything happens for a reason, and remember to look back in our lives, we will grow and build a legacy others can learn from.

I practice looking back at my successes to stay motivated for the future. I was around 7 years old at Carver Elementary, when I shifted from receiving "Most Improved Student" awards to "Academic Achievement" awards. Memories of middle school are slowly diminishing. Throughout all years attending Willowbrook Middle School, "Perfect Attendance" awards were normal for me; doctor and dentist appointments were the only exceptions. King/Drew Magnet High School of Medicine and Science was a life changing and invigorating experience. Getting accepted to the school was an accomplishment within itself. I maintained a 3.0 GPA while participating in the school's play *SUENOS*, which means "Dreams" in Spanish. From that performance I obtained the ability to be more confident in myself and to do what I thought was right for me. Throughout 2010 successes came back to back. At the end of high school I was crowned King at Prom and enhanced my relationships with my previous teachers and community leaders. Then I was accepted to "CSUN" and received many scholarships from the Department of Children and Family Services, which provided me with financial support for my full-time college experience. In March, 2010 I ran the Los Angeles Marathon from the Dodger Stadium to the Santa Monica Pier. Pounding the pavement with my size 9 and a half pair of K-Swiss shoes and my heavy breathing was like riding the elevator to heaven. I vividly remember the feeling of food deprivation, dehydration and exhaustion. Nonetheless, the skies were filled with the air of success and after I passed the finished line to receive my medal, I thanked God. ☺ I imported every lesson I learned from that experience. I learned to keep persevering even when it hurts, rise above all obstacles to succeed and to always finish what I started and believed. I also ran the Aids Walk in October of 2010, and held a leading role in another theatrical production in South L.A. with a diverse group of teenagers in July, 2010. All accomplishments concluded as life lessons.

This journey better known as college is a metaphor for life. Though we are all striving for a better life in a sense, or a degree, we are to grow through trial and error and make decisions that could potentially benefit us in the future. I always tried to be myself, but I have to say it is harder than it seems. I don't know my family history and I share an identity with my identical twin. As I've grown I've had the reputation of being meek, personable, enthusiastic and helpful. I want my family and loved ones to remember me as the young man who surpassed all negative impediments and succeeded further than the expectations of others. I also wish to be remembered by my love ones as an aspiring actor and poet. I'm not sure if my dreams of becoming an actor will ever become reality, but I have a bit of optimism. ☺ Anyone who knows me knows that I love to perform and be the center of attention. Ultimately, I would like to be remembered as a child of God. I've been enhancing my relationship with the Lord and will be one beacon of light that did what I was sent here on earth to do. Passionately following his word, I tend to realize, being normal in our eyes is not being normal in God's eyes. Whether a person believes in God or not, I say faith exists in everyone. Beliefs are morals that guide people.

I believe the God is Love and God is my Lord and savior. Though I don't always go to church or clarify myself as Christian, I still have a close companionship with God. There are many answers in the Bible that assist me in the direction I'd like to take in life. I will forever have an identity crisis until I find my identity in God. He is the reason why I exist and why I follow my passions.

I see myself as a leader in the upcoming years. I aim to start and manage an inspirational company that will benefit children in distress situations and youth who are faced with unexpected adversities. Though my life has only begun to positively turn around, I am sure many bumps in the road will try to slow me down. I will continue to drive toward the light and pick up as many hitch hikers that are on their way to success as well. If I were to leave this earth today, my epitaph would read:

> *I am not defined by my successes, but the failures it took to get to where I am.*

My family friends and experiences are the reasons why I am sagacious, responsible and independent. I owe my life to everyone around me, for their impact on my growth. ☺ If it was from my first Love, Danae Odom, who taught me that leaving isn't always a bad choice. My best friend from Willowbrook, Gracia Alonso, taught me life moves on, and those by your side throughout your journey of failures and successes are the people who should be valued. I am thankful.

We Were Raised From Scratch

In 1992 dreams and legends were born.
The wisest of the wise were raised like corn and taught,
Not to steal just ask, not to cry just laugh, and not to hate, but to love those
who hated them.

We were Raised From Scratch

If we were all color blind, our skin tones would say the least about us.
Our ideas wouldn't be dreams without us and our dreams would reserve big
lots on the right side of our brains to change the realm of reality.
We're able to grow smooth like hickory, and strong like bamboo,

We use our abilities to do our best and teach the rest, that the youth in our
community will be better than any blessing, that we could ever ask for.
We own ventriloquist visions,
they talk to us because we were taught to only speak when we're spoken to.

We were Raised From Scratch

Snuggies don't exist to us because we don't relax, we're different, we wear
hijabs of wisdom and ties of knowledge to offer racks on racks on racks of
nutrition to raise those beneath us.

We were Raised From Scratch
We were built to last
We were taught to share
We were punished for coming in last

An actor once told me, 100 no's will shatter us, and only 1 yes will make us
proceed to success.

One last note, Never digress!

Don't take the shortcuts because patience can make our journeys as long as
the great wall of China,
We shall never give up because as long as we're breathing the same air as
god, we won't let distress situations dry us out like the Sahara desert because
in this life we must finish the race in order to win it.
So we live it, live with cold nights, lived with no lights, lived with nothing but
beans, and live with faith for our blurry dreams.

You can take our styles, but you will never be able to take the fact that we were Raised From Scratch.

My full family today...

- My twin Demontray and I are currently EOP-Resilient Scholars at California State University, Northridge. He is pursuing Business Finance and I am pursuing two majors, Business Management and Communications. We both have the same cars and are contemplating on starting a company together.
- My sister Keke is pursuing a nursing degree and stays in Lancaster, Ca.
- My brother Joey is 21 and lives in Compton, Ca.
- Uncle Lowe is still traveling to Arkansas every year and holding strong. He seems to be in better health than expected.
- My mother, who I have not held a conversation with for 10 years until this book, Beatrice Ophelia Carruthers, is currently staying in an apartment in the South L.A. area.
- My father has 13 kids in total and is serving time in prison. He is expected to be released sometime soon.
- Thalia Thompson, my dad's oldest child, is someone I have yet to meet.
- My step-sister and brothers are Jasmine (age 7), Daveion (age 5), Traveontae (age 4) are my dad's youngest children.
- Alisha M. Harrell is my oldest sister. She has 3 kids, Layla (age 7), Daisya and Kamron (ages 15). She is a single mom who loves and supports her son and two daughters.
- My sister Quannice, has a daughter, Alise Brooks, who has autism. Quannice is 27 and stays in Lancaster, Ca.
- My sister Shanta has a baby boy by the name of Coryion (age 6). She is 25 year old and is a single mom and hair stylist, lives in Los Angeles, Ca.
- My brother Justin 23 serving 13year in mill creek prison no kids
- My sister Quiron is 17 and is serving 3months in penitentiary.

➢ My oldest brother Gary, has a baby boy by the name of Gary Jr. (age 5), and is now a manager at his current job, and he is living in Lancaster, Ca.

Seemingly our family is working together to build stronger bonds with communication over the phone, and through celebratory events and reunions.

Current posts and updates about my family will be on my blog http://raisedfromscratch.tumblr.com/

I also urge you to following me on Twitter @Raised4rmSctratch and "Like" my Facebook fan page: Raised From Scratch

(it's not the end...to be continued...)

Acknowledgements and Thanks

"Stand for him or fall for anything...though I aint good enough he still loves me." *–He Still Loves Me* by Beyonce

I would like to give total praise to my maker. Thanks you GOD I could not have done it without your grace.
Lorenzo Edwards (Uncle Lowe) I owe you all my success and accomplishments.
I give appreciation to my guardian angels who have fought for me to be where I am.
Verna May Edwards (Great Auntie), Vernistine Thompson (Grandma)

Demontray Thompson, without you I could not go on. You motivate and encourage me to stay focused. I hope you enjoy this book.

To my dear brothers, sisters, aunties, uncles, cousins and lost friends I thank you from the bottom of my heart for your contributions to my life.

A special thanks to Dr. Shani Byard, Message Media Ed – School of Black Leadership in the Digital Age, for offering the Digital Scholars Book Writing & Publishing program, the guidelines and support for writing this book. Without your talented support this book would cease to exist. I'd also like to thank the guest speakers for the Digital Scholars program: Duzac, Alice "the poet" Nicholas, Theo Fowles, and Joanne Griffith-Poplar for your advice and sponsorship of my bookmarks!

Much appreciation to my cover artist, Rachael Dinsmore.

I give special appreciation for knowledge obtained from the communities at Cal State University, Northridge, King/Drew Magnet High School of Medicine and Science, Willowbrook Middle School and George Washington Carver Elementary.

Ultimately, I thank my friends, co-workers, esteemed supporters and readers for your diligent care and assistance through my journey.

I give respectful apologizes to those who should be on this list, but are not mentioned.

49

Made in the USA
Middletown, DE
18 November 2015